I am a

BUDDHIST

I am a

BUDDHIST

Dhanapala Samarasekara
and
Udeni Samarasekara

Photography: Chris Fairclough

Religious Consultant: Ven. Dr. H. Saddhatissa

FRANKLIN WATTS

LONDON/NEW YORK/SYDNEY/TORONTO

Udeni Samarasekara is ten years old.
She and her family are Buddhists.
Her father, Dhanapala, is a former
diplomat. Her mother, Parvathy
Thevy, is a doctor. Udeni has two
sisters: Manjula who is nineteen, and
Vidhisha who is fourteen. Udeni's
parents came to England from Sri
Lanka in 1967 and now live in Ilford,
Essex, England.

Contents

© 1986 Watts Books
Paperback edition 1993
This edition 1995

Watts Books
96 Leonard Street
London
EC2A 4RH

Franklin Watts Australia
14 Mars Road
Lane Cove
NSW 2066

ISBN 0 86313 261 8 (hardback)
ISBN 0 7496 1407 2 (paperback)

The Publishers would like to thank the Samarasekara family and all others shown in this book.

Printed in Italy

The Buddhist belief

My family follows the teachings of the Buddha. Many things in our house remind us of our religion.

Prince Siddhartha Gautama, who became the Buddha, was born in India about 560 BC. Until he was 28 he lived a life of luxury. By chance he saw that the lives of most people were full of hardships and suffering. He decided to go in search of wisdom. After several years he came to understand the meaning of life.

The Buddha has given us many thoughts about how to live our lives.

Buddhists follow the "Eightfold path" which is a set of guidelines to lead the right sort of life by avoiding all extremes. Buddha taught that we undergo many lives on this earth until we reach, through our own effort, a state of perfect peace called "Nirvana". The Buddha was in his final lifetime when he became enlightened. The name Buddha means "Enlightened One."

Going to the Temple

We go to the Temple whenever we can. A flag flies over our Temple.

Buddhists do not have to go to the Temple at any special time or day. It is however common to do so on the Full-Moon day. A Buddhist Temple is called a Vihara. In a Temple there is usually a shrine room with a large image of the Buddha and statues of his disciples. There are also Buddhist relics and manuscripts of the Buddha's teaching. There is also a lecture room, a library, and a meditation room at the Vihara.

We have to take our shoes off
when we go into the Temple. We
also light candles and incense
sticks.

Buddhists remove their shoes as a
mark of respect to Buddha. They
regard the Buddha, not as a god, but
as a great teacher. They light candles
and sweet smelling incense sticks as a
tribute to the Buddha. While they are
doing these things, Buddhists usually
recite special verses.

Temple Customs

We make offerings of flowers and food to the Buddha.

When Buddhists place flowers or food before the statue of the Buddha they usually recite "gathas" or verses. These remind them that their own bodies, like the flowers, will not last forever. People also offer gifts of food and other things to the monks, since they have nothing of their own. Buddhists feel that giving a gift is an action which helps them achieve their Nirvana.

Our Monks have shaved heads and wear the same robes as the Buddha's first followers.

One ceremony which takes place at the Temple almost every day is "Dana" which is the offering of food to the monks. They do not eat after noon, so the offering must be made before that time. Sometimes monks are invited to people's homes for Dana. On such occasions people give robes and other needs to the monks. The monks give the people their blessings in return.

The Buddhist Way

The monks chant verses from the Holy books. They do this in our home on special occasions.

The chanting of sacred passages or Pirith, has been a custom since the Buddha's time. It marks the end of many ceremonies and some families chant Pirith before going to bed each night. The Buddha's sermons, or "Sutras," are felt to have a special importance or power. On special occasions the chanting goes on, without a break, for several days.

The monks help us to understand the message of the Buddha. Sometimes they tie a Holy Thread on our wrists.

Homage, or "Vandana," is made to the Buddha, his teaching and his monks. This is followed by meditation or deep thinking on a special theme. This is a very important part of the Buddhist Way. The theme of the meditation can be something like "loving kindness." The Holy Thread tied to the wrists at the end of some ceremonies is thought to protect a person from all evil.

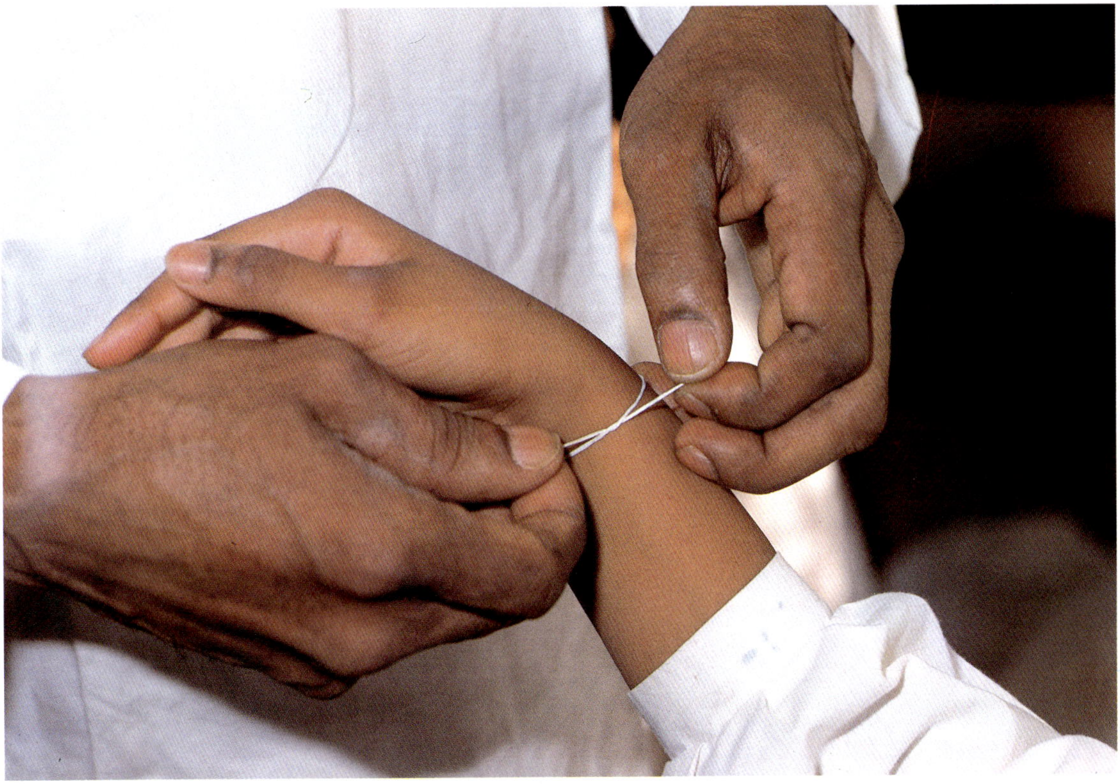

We have a Buddha image at home. We take the Five Vows in front of it every day.

Many Buddhists follow the practice of repeating the Five Vows every day. In these Vows, Buddhists promise not to harm any living thing, not to take anything which is not given to them, not to misuse their senses, not to speak wrongly, and not to use drugs or intoxicating drinks. It is not enough just to make these promises: a Buddhist must live by them as well.

I would like to learn the meaning of the different positions of the Buddha in his images.

When the Buddha is shown with his right hand pointing downward, it is said to represent his triumph over earthly temptations. Another pose, showing him with his fingers near his heart and the palms touching, represents the Buddha when he was preaching his first sermon. The same postures are found in images of the Buddha all over the world but the face of the Buddha often differs in different countries.

The Holy Books

I like to read the many stories about the life of Buddha.

The Buddha's main teachings are found in the "Tripitaka" or "Three Baskets." They consist of thirty-one books divided into three sections dealing with three different aspects of the Buddha's teaching. One of the books, written in verse, is the "Dhammapada," which gives examples from over 500 stories about the life of the Buddha. Each has a moral and they are often used in sermons by monks.

The Holy Books of Buddhism are written in the Pali language, which comes from India.

From the time of the Buddha, temples have been places of education. All have large libraries of religious books, some in Pali, and some translated into the native language of the country. Many children attend Sunday school at the Vihara to learn about Buddhism. The Buddha's teachings were first written down quite a long time after he died. They are written on palm leaves.

The Pāli alphabet in Sinhalese characters

Vowels

ඇ = a   ඈ = á   ඉ = i   ඊ = í
උ = u   ඌ = ú   ඒ = ē   ඕ = ō

Consonants

ක = ka   ඛ = kha   ග = ġa   ඝ = gha
ඞ = na   ච = ca   ඡ = cha   ජ = ja
ඣ = jha   ඤ = ña   ට = ta   ඨ = tha
ඩ = da   ඪ = dha   ණ = ni
ත = ta   ථ = tha   ද = da   ධ = dha
න = na   ප = pa   ඵ = pha   බ = ba
භ = bha   ම = ma

ය = ya   ර = ra   ල = la   ව = va
ස = sa   හ = ha   ළ = la   ං = m

The history of Udeni's family

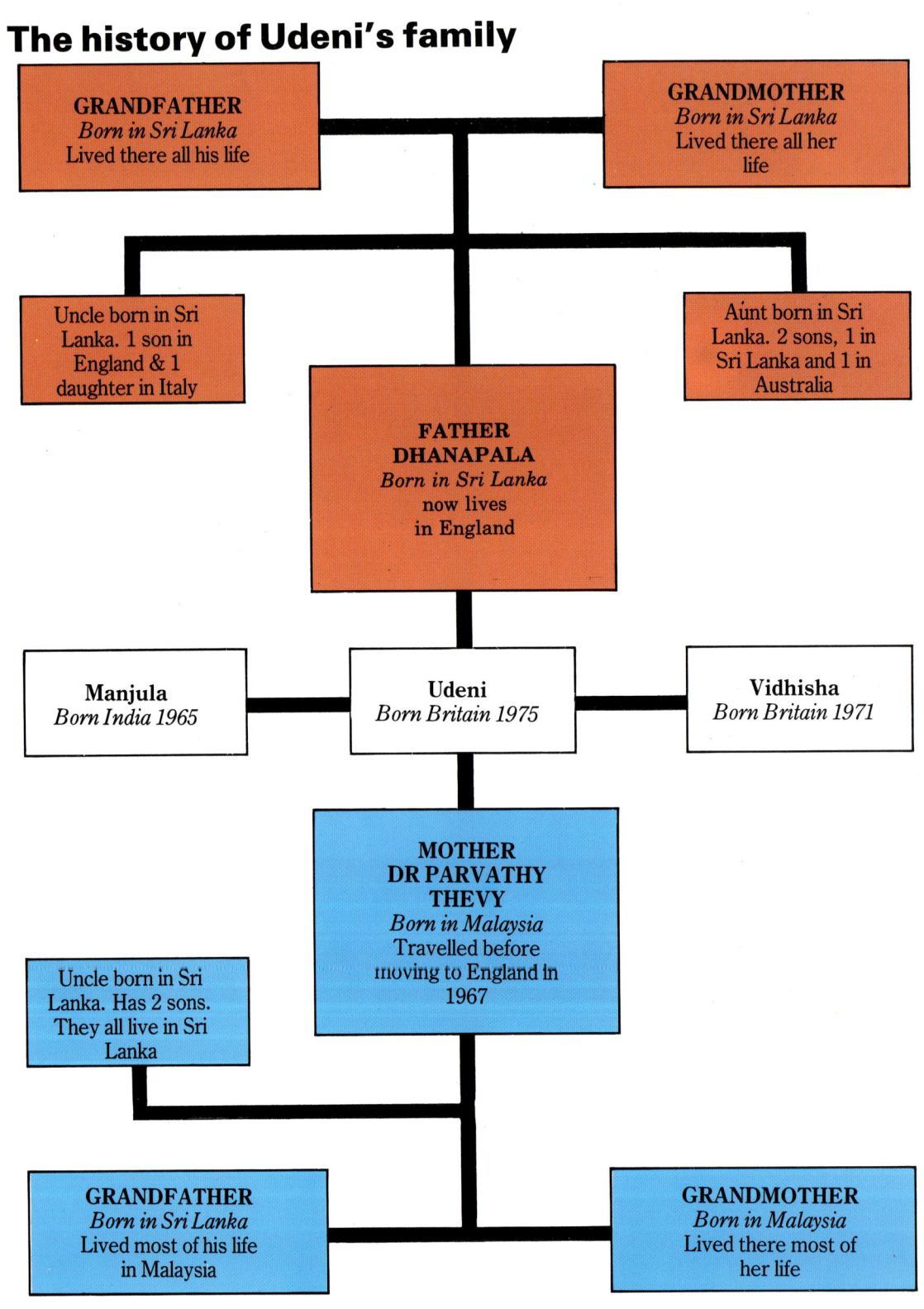

GRANDFATHER
Born in Sri Lanka
Lived there all his life

GRANDMOTHER
Born in Sri Lanka
Lived there all her life

Uncle born in Sri Lanka. 1 son in England & 1 daughter in Italy

Aunt born in Sri Lanka. 2 sons, 1 in Sri Lanka and 1 in Australia

**FATHER
DHANAPALA**
Born in Sri Lanka
now lives
in England

Manjula
Born India 1965

Udeni
Born Britain 1975

Vidhisha
Born Britain 1971

**MOTHER
DR PARVATHY
THEVY**
Born in Malaysia
Travelled before moving to England in 1967

Uncle born in Sri Lanka. Has 2 sons. They all live in Sri Lanka

GRANDFATHER
Born in Sri Lanka
Lived most of his life in Malaysia

GRANDMOTHER
Born in Malaysia
Lived there most of her life

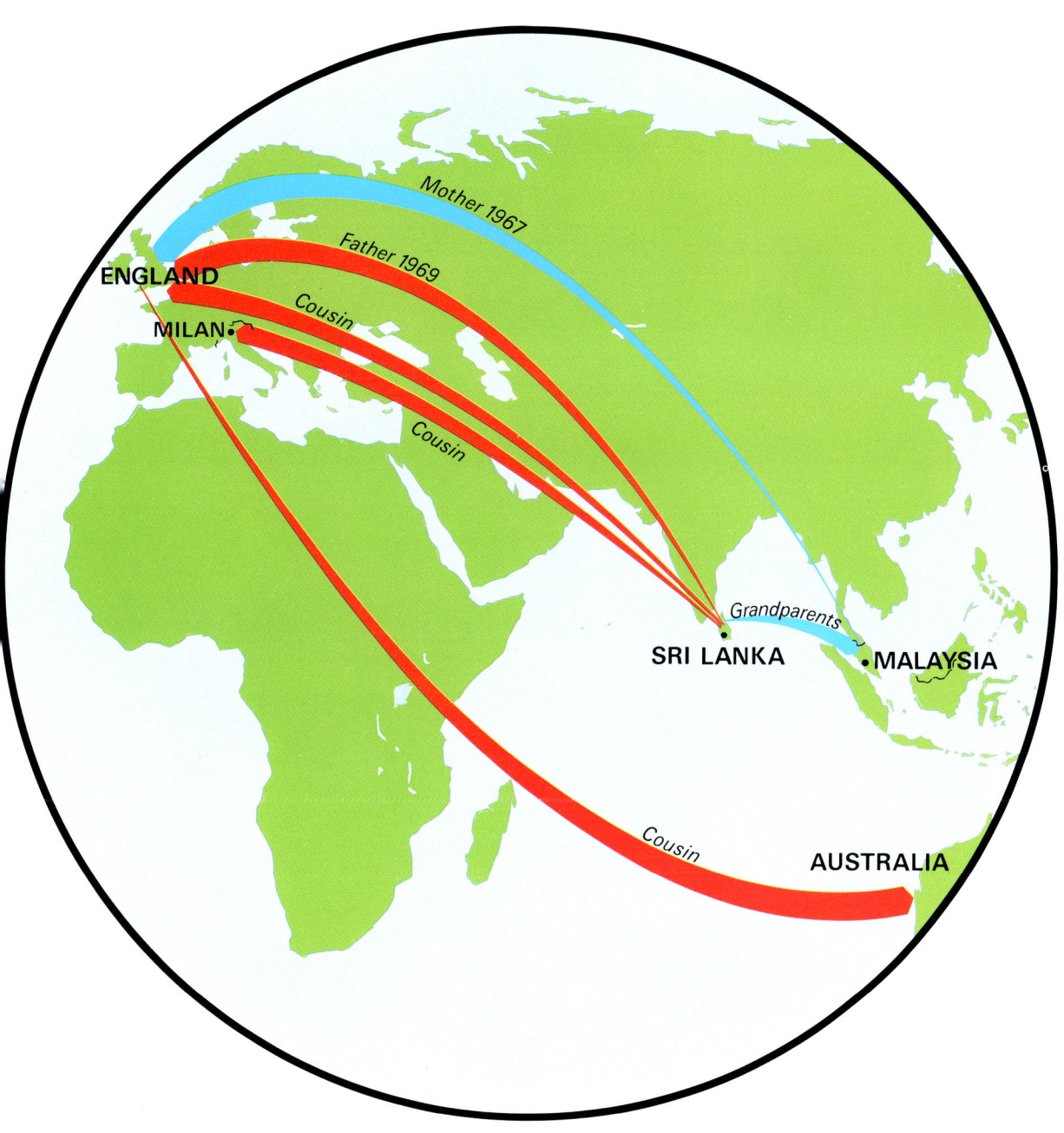

ENGLAND

MILAN

Mother 1967

Father 1969

Cousin

Cousin

Grandparents

SRI LANKA

MALAYSIA

Cousin

AUSTRALIA

19

Cooking and Eating

I enjoy choosing the special vegetables we use in our cooking.

Some Buddhists are vegetarians. They follow a strict diet and eat no meat, fish or eggs. Diet is, however, really a matter of personal choice, like everything else in Buddhism. Udeni's family often eats the mildly curried food which is typical of Sri Lanka. On Full-Moon days, they prefer to eat only vegetarian food.

I love my mother's cooking. We often have yogurt for desert, topped with syrup.

There are no forbidden foods for Buddhists, so families eat whatever food is the custom in their country. Udeni's family comes from Sri Lanka and many of their dishes are from that country. Main meals often consist of mildly curried meat and vegetable dishes with boiled rice. They have many dessert dishes, such as rice cakes.

What a Buddhist wears

My mother makes most of the clothes I wear. I have some lovely Sri Lankan dresses.

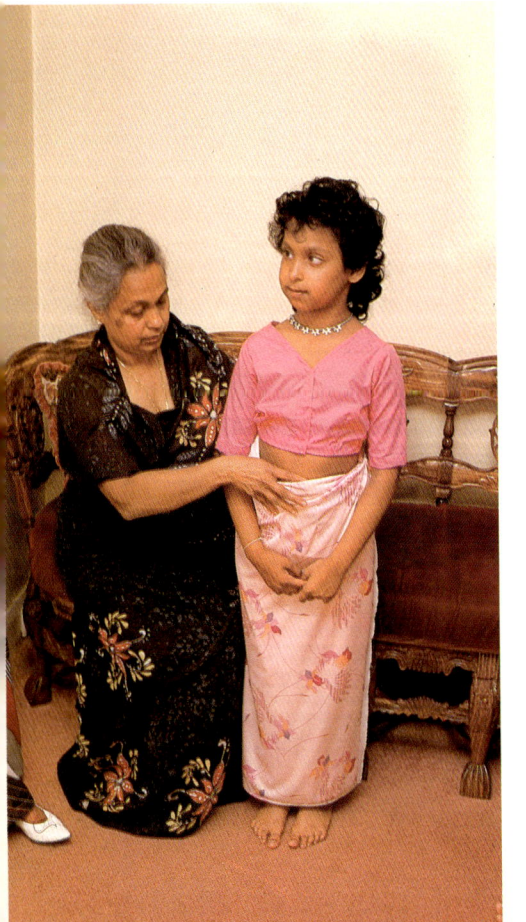

Women usually wear the national dress of the country from which they come. This can be either a sari or a "cloth and jacket." Men in Britain usually wear European clothes. The Sari is a single piece of cloth up to six yards in length, worn with a blouse. The cloth is a skirt made of up to three yards of material. The jacket is like a short-sleeved blouse.

On Full-Moon days we wear simple white clothes when we visit the Temple.

On the Full-Moon days many Buddhists observe the "Attha-Sila" or Eight Vows. These consist of the Five Vows which are taken every day plus three more, in which they promise not to eat after midday, not to dance or sing, use perfume or other things which "adorn and beautify the person," and not to use luxurious beds and chairs. It is customary to wear simple white clothes.

A Buddhist Wedding

I look forward to weddings. They are always very exciting.

Many Buddhist marriages are arranged by the parents of the bride and groom. Parents arrange for suitable sons and daughters to meet. An engagement and wedding are agreed upon if they accept each other. Astrologers advise about the best days for engagements and weddings. The wedding ceremony is not performed by a Buddhist monk or in a Temple. It is held at home or a hotel.

**The best part of a
wedding is the Poruwa ceremony
and the feast afterward.**

The Bride and Groom are led on to the
Poruwa by the Bride's uncle. The
Poruwa is a platform which has been
beautifully decorated with white
flowers. There they exchange rings,
and the thumbs of their right hands
are tied together by the Bride's uncle.
During this time there is chanting
from the Buddhist scriptures. The
feasting and celebrating goes on for
several days.

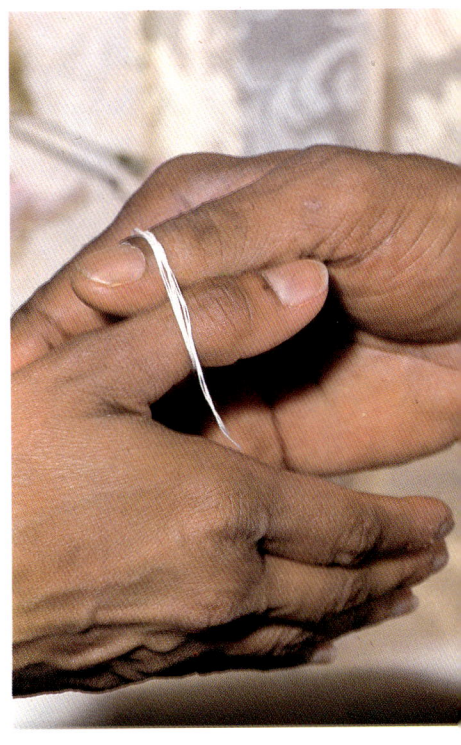

Festivals and shrines

I was given a ceremonial mask when I visited Sri Lanka. I saw the Kandy Perahera.

In countries with very large Buddhist populations there are impressive processions on Full-Moon days. In Sri Lanka the festival of the August Moon, called the Kandy Perahera, is the most famous. It is held in the city of Kandy. Over one hundred elephants and many drummers and dancers go in procession.

I have visited some of the beautiful shrines found in Sri Lanka and seen huge statues of the Buddha.

The Temple of the Tooth, seen above, is among the oldest and most sacred shrines in Sri Lanka. A tooth of the Buddha was brought to Sri Lanka hundreds of years ago. In India there are several sacred places associated with the life and teachings of the Buddha. In other Buddhist countries there are many famous and beautiful temples and statues, such as that at Polonnaruwa in Sri Lanka, seen here.

The Buddhist Year

Buddhists use the lunar calendar. The first month of the year is Vesakha as the Buddha was born on this Full-Moon Day. Each Full-Moon day has a special significance which may differ from country to country. Shown here are those observed in Sri Lanka.

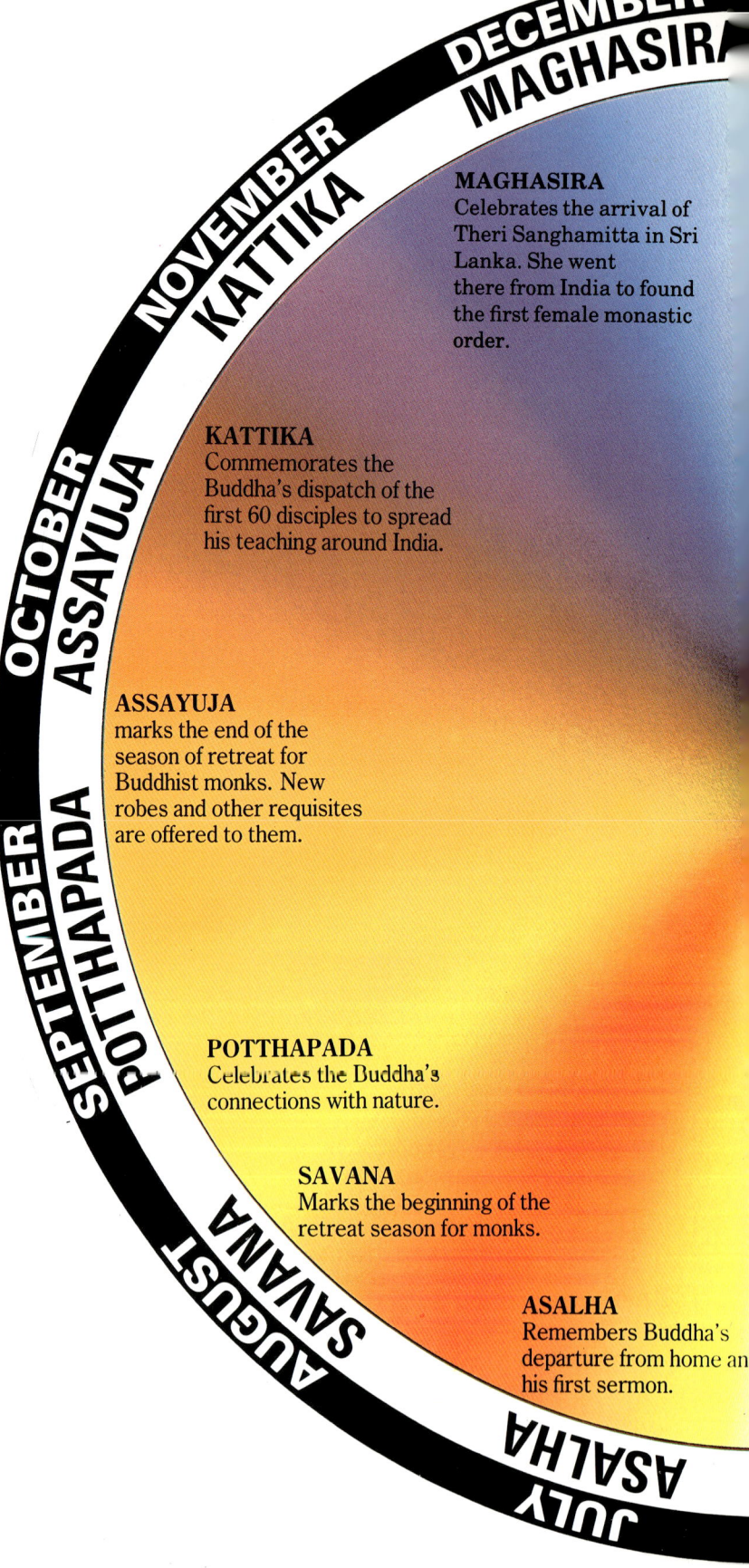

MAGHASIRA
Celebrates the arrival of Theri Sanghamitta in Sri Lanka. She went there from India to found the first female monastic order.

KATTIKA
Commemorates the Buddha's dispatch of the first 60 disciples to spread his teaching around India.

ASSAYUJA
marks the end of the season of retreat for Buddhist monks. New robes and other requisites are offered to them.

POTTHAPADA
Celebrates the Buddha's connections with nature.

SAVANA
Marks the beginning of the retreat season for monks.

ASALHA
Remembers Buddha's departure from home and his first sermon.

DECEMBER MAGHASIRA
NOVEMBER KATTIKA
OCTOBER ASSAYUJA
SEPTEMBER POTTHAPADA
AUGUST SAVANA
JULY ASALHA

JANUARY
PHUSSA

PHUSSA
Celebrates the Buddha's
legendary first visit to Sri
Lanka.

FEBRUARY
MAGHA

MAGHA
Commemorates Buddha's
giving the title of Chief
Disciple to both Sariputta
and Moggallana.

PHAGGUNA
Marks Buddha's return to
his birth place of
Kapilavastu and the
conversion of his family to
Buddhism.

MARCH
PHAGGUNA

CHITTAMASA
Celebrates the role of
Buddha as a peacemaker.

APRIL
CHITTAMASA

VESAKHA
This is the most important
festival in the year and
marks the birth,
enlightenment and death of
Buddha.

VESAKHA
MAY

JETTHAMASA
Commemorates the spread
of Buddhism from India to
other countries.

JETTHAMASA
JUNE

29

Facts and figures

There are thought to be about 1,000 million Buddhists in the world today, and they are found in nearly every country. Of these, about 700 million are found in communist states such as China, North Korea and Viet Nam.

About 60,000 Buddhists live in Great Britain. Most of them came originally from Sri Lanka, India, China, Burma or Tibet. There are over 200,000 in the United States who came mainly from China and Japan.

There are many different Buddhist sects or groups, but they fall into two main catergories. The Mahayana Buddhists spread northward from the birthplace of the Buddha, into China, Mongolia, Korea, Japan, Tibet and Viet Nam. This group includes the Zen Buddhists of Japan. The other group, called the Theravada Buddhists, are thought to keep more closely to the original teachings of the Buddha. Theravada Buddhism spread southward into Sri Lanka, Burma, Thailand, Laos and Kampuchea

Buddha's followers went out to preach the Four Noble Truths and the Eightfold Path, journeyed far and wide during the Indian dry season, but during the rainly season they lived together in one place, preaching to nearby villages. This life as a community developed into the orders of Buddhist monks with which we are familiar today. They generally wear saffron yellow robes and have shaved heads. They carry a begging bowl, for food, clothing and other necessities.

The Buddha's teaching followed by the main branches of Buddhism are: The Four Noble Truths:–
– All life contains suffering.
– Suffering is caused by our selfish attachment to the things of the world.
– We can escape from the suffering by rejecting worldly things.
– The way to do this is by avoiding all extremes in life.

This can be avoided by following the 'Eightfold Path':–
– Right Understanding;
– Right Intention;
– Right Speech;
– Right Conduct;
– Right Occupation;
– Right Endeavor;
– Right Contemplation;
– Right Concentration;

Glossary

Attha-Sila The eight vows (Promises) made on the conduct of life by Buddhists. They are usually made on Full-Moon Days.

Buddha The name given to Prince Siddhartha Gautama after he came to understand the meaning of life. Means "Enlightened One."

Dana The giving of alms (gifts) to monks, the poor or needy.

Eightfold Path The main teaching of Buddhism which tells how to end all suffering and achieve salvation.

Enlightenment The highest spiritual aim of all Buddhists when one is "awakened" into a state of peace and freedom from impurities such as greed and ignorance.

Four Noble Truths The Buddhist description of the nature of life and how peace and happiness can be achieved.

Full-Moon Day The Buddhist holy day, each month, on which special events are celebrated.

Gathas Verses recited during Buddhist worship.

Meditation The way in which a Buddhist disciplines and purifies the mind. It is a very important practice in the Buddhist belief.

Middle Path The avoiding of all extremes of thought and action in life.

Nirvana The last stage of the life cycle when a person achieves complete salvation. A state of supreme happiness.

Pali The language used in the Holy Books. The Buddha preached in Pali, the language of the masses in order to reach the most people.

Pirith The ceremony of chanting from the Holy Books by monks to give blessings and protection to all.

Poruwa The platform decorated with white flowers onto which the bride and groom are led for the wedding ceremony.

Sutra The sermons of the Buddha.

Vandana Homage made to the Buddha, his teaching and the monks.

Vihara A Buddhist temple or monastery in which monks are found.

Index